A New You!

Letting Go of the Past

Trusting God with our Future

by New Way Today

Scripture quotations are taken mostly from the New American Bible, St. Joseph's Edition copyright © 1970 by the Confraternity of Christian Doctrine, and the Holy Bible, New International Version.

The thoughts, opinions, and beliefs expressed in this book are those of New Way Today.

Published by Kathleen Hammer
ISBN-13:978-1494203191
ISBN-10:1494203197

Author website information:

www.newwaytoday.net
www.facebook.com/NewWayToday

I dedicate this book to my parents
who introduced me to God,

and to God Himself,
who knows how often I fail to live up to everything
I write here, but who also knows how hard I try...
and will keep trying.

Introduction

It's time. We've put it off long enough. The past has taken up too much space in our hearts and minds. It has too much influence in our lives and in our relationships. The past robs us of the present and it's time to release it. It's time to begin again.

Everyone needs a fresh start. In New Way Today's *"A New You"*, we will seek the inner healing our souls crave and attempt to rejuvenate our personal and spiritual life through a deeper understanding of God's Love for us.

We will restore our emotional life by giving ourselves permission to let go of the past and surrender our future into the arms of a loving God. God wants to do something *New* with our lives. When we hold onto the past, keeping it alive, we deny ourselves a better life and rob ourselves of inner peace and joy.

Our old way hasn't worked, and now we know it. Our own efforts have not brought us the happiness we seek. The things we have done to try and heal ourselves hasn't worked either. Our attempts have not produced results and we are still in need of emotional healing. It's time for a New Way. It's time for God's Way.

Change isn't easy. Starting a new life by letting go of pain is a challenge. But remaining in pain is an even greater one. We have a God of Love and Mercy who wants to show us that when we turn situations over to Him, He will bring us a life of peace and happiness that we never saw coming.

God can make us a *new creation*, if we let Him. He can bring us the healing we seek. He can restore what is broken, but it starts with us. We need to be open to His grace and healing Love. God understands our pain. He's not indifferent to it. He knows it's difficult to let go, and by now, we know it too. We know what we have to do, but we're stuck. We need to surrender and forgive, but it's hard. We know we have to move forward - but we don't want to.

The heart and soul of New Way Today was built upon the scripture found in Isaiah 43:18-19, *"Remember not the events of the past ... I am doing something New!"* Through this scripture we come to the understanding that God truly doesn't want to remember our past anymore and He doesn't want us to either. This doesn't mean that what has happened in our past has not been very serious or very painful. It does mean that we have a God who wants to *free us* from this pain. We have a God who cares about us, who was with us then, and is with us still.

When we come to know God as our loving Father, we, above all, find a safe place. A place where we are protected, where we can rest from our feelings. He is our *"hiding place." (Psalm 32:7)* It's a place where healing is possible because we don't have to pretend anymore. God will love and accept us as we are.

In the unthreatened setting of God's Love, we are free to be ourselves, our real selves, who desire to be loved and cared for in the deepest way possible. When we reach this place we are able to let our guard down and let Love in. That's when change happens. The Love of God is the change that we need.

One night I picked up a pen and without much thinking wrote the prayer that you'll see at the start of this book called *A New Way.* It was simple and from the heart, and very unexpected. With this prayer came the understanding that we all need to start over. No matter what your past or present situation, each of us needs to be renewed. Every day we can be better people than we were the day before.

9

New Way Today's *"A New You"*, follows a basic pattern of short chapters beginning with a scripture or quote, followed by reflection, then a prayer. At the end of each chapter there are reflection questions, where we can really examine our own unique situation through a private and honest dialogue with God. We can talk with God in prayer about the answers. God already knows our past and He already loves us. He understands what we've been through and what we are going through now. We can be open with Him when answering these questions and have a real "heart to heart" with Jesus. You won't shock Him. There's nothing you can say that He doesn't already know, and He already Loves you to death!

To get the most out of this book, it can also be combined with New Way Today's *"My New Way Journal."* There is power in the pen, and writing down our *"new way"* of doing things and our goals for the future, has its own healing aspect. It's a daily journal for the calendar year that is yours to document your own unique emotional and spiritual growth. No one knows your situation better than you and God, and together you can become *A New You*! This book and the journal complement each other and it is through this joint effort that we will see encouraging results.

This book will have no proof for you of God's existence, and it will not discuss any great theological topics. It will, however, speak to those who need it. It's a book for your spirit, to be read with your heart and listened to with your soul, and God will do the rest.

It's the sort of book that never gets old, as each chapter will speak to you again at different times of your life. The insights in "*A New You*" are short and simple, but hopefully you find it helpful, prayerful and worthwhile. It's not an elaborate book, and it's far from perfect, but a *New You* has the potential to emerge, while allowing God, the author of Love, to direct the course of our lives from now on.

We all have choices. Taking this step towards personal and spiritual growth is a good one. I hope this book will bring healing and peace to you. I hope you will discover a new way of seeing things, a new way of doing things, a new attitude towards life which will motivate you to live more fully in the present moment.

Above all, I hope you will have a New understanding of God's unconditional and tender love for you and everyone in your life. I hope this new understanding fills your spirit and frees you to become a new and better version of yourself, free from the past and unafraid of the future, by God's grace.

You're not alone. God is with you. Our Creator has not forgotten us. He cares. He Loves. He Heals. He forgives. This is what He does. It's who He is. He can't be anything else. He never gets tired of giving us second chances. God is Love and we are in good hands.

Let's walk with Him now, safe and sound, loved and protected, allowing Him to guide our steps and hold our hand as we leave the past behind and say *Yes* to our future. You don't have to wait any longer. You can have a New life, as *A New You*, in a *New Way ... Today!*

Lord, grant me ...

A new Way....

A new way of Living

A new way of Loving

A new way of Thinking

A new way of Speaking

A new way of Believing

A new way of Hoping

A new way of Seeing

A new way of Hearing

A new way of Communicating

A new way of Feeling

A new way of Trusting

A new way of Praying

A New Me

A me who follows you once and for all, and forever!

Amen

Chapter 1

Remember not the events of the past, the things of long ago consider not; See, I am doing something new!

~ Isaiah 43:18-19

The past is over.

Let's listen to this sentence softly. Without judgment or condemnation, hear this gentle truth whisper into our souls. A truth we already know but maybe haven't accepted. Let's allow this reality to sink in without any negativity, explanations, or advice from others. Let's listen to this sentence as we are wrapped in the arms of our loving God. Hear it spoken with Love. Safe and sound, hear it peacefully, but hear it clearly. The past is over.

Now hear that it's ok. Wherever we are at this moment in our emotional and spiritual journey, we have a loving God carrying us by His grace, and because of that - everything will be all right. It may not feel that way yet, but our hearts know there's more out there but we can't get to it because we're stuck.

It's ok to let the past go, primarily because it doesn't even exist. It's not there. Actually, it's been gone for a while now. Only in our mind, where we have been keeping it alive, does the past play a role and become part of our present. It is our remembering that opens the sore over and over again, not giving the wound time to heal. In this

15

scripture we hear God speaking to us. It's remembering that seems to be the problem.

The definition of the word "remember" is "to recall to *the mind by an act or effort"* ... *"to retain in memory"* ... *"to keep in mind"* and *"remain aware of".* I don't know about you but I hear a lot of action words there.

Sometimes we are so accustomed to re-living old memories and conversations in our head that we forget we can choose what we think about. It becomes so automatic, as if our thoughts are just something that happens to us. They're not. We are in control of the process. We choose what we think about.

What happened to us is not what's under our control, it's no longer under anyone's control. It's not there anymore. People are responsible for their behavior, but really, there is nothing anyone can do about the past. No one can go back in time. Yet we try to, day after day, hoping something will change this time. Our thoughts are under our control, and our Lord gently teaches us in this scripture, to think about something else.

How do we let go of the past when it still brings us pain? How do we do what God asks, to not remember it anymore? I mean, that sounds kind of dismissive. At first, we may feel like putting God in the boat with everyone else who tells us to "get over it already". Something we obviously haven't been able to do yet, not completely anyway.

So why would we hold on to something that isn't there? We stay attached to what isn't, and why - because it's too painful not to. It hurts to let it go. It feels like we are losing some kind of a friend. The past has been safe and reliable, but when your pain becomes greater than your comfort level you know you need to do something about it.

It feels like you are going to lose something if you let go of the past, but that's just a feeling. You will lose nothing because it's already been gone. You will just come to accept it and in doing so you will gain everything.

The truth is that the past is not a friend, it's a foe. It keeps us stuck. It keeps us sad. It freezes us and holds us back. We are afraid to leave it and afraid to stay with it. The good news ... the past is in our mind. Our thoughts keep us there and our thoughts can change. We can change our attitude and choose the right words to say to ourselves. I'm sure if you're reading this type of book, you've heard this before, but hear it again in a *New Way.* Be open to letting it sink in this time.

In this scripture verse, God clearly tells us to stop thinking about it. "Remember *not* the events of the past." Do not even consider the past anymore. Trust that God is a lot smarter than we are and He knows what He's doing. Trust that He wouldn't tell us to forget the past if it was good for us to keep remembering it. It isn't. It's destructive. God knows it and we know it too.

The problem is how do we stop thinking about the past when we are deeply hurt by it, when it has consumed us for so long? The answer is always the same - prayer. Talk to

God. Tell Him how hard this is for you. Tell Him your past still has a hold on you, in whatever way you want to.

We can ask God for the grace to let the past go. We don't have to do it alone. He will help us. He has a gentle way with these things. He knows your situation. He will guide you step by step safely through the process. God Loves You. Trust Him. Hold onto Him. He will not let you fall.

We are in need of God's healing love. He has something new in store for us. Something new is waiting. He knows we can't receive it if we are still holding onto something else. So be assured He wants to help you. Empty your heart to God now, give Him your wounds, your memories, your forgotten hopes, your sins, your broken dreams, your fears of the future, and allow Him to take it and make your life new.

Say *Yes* to God! Let Him do what He wants. Give Him permission. Let God love you. Let God hold you. Let God help you. Let God free you. Let God console you. Let God strengthen you. Let God guard your heart for you. Let God into your life. Let go of the pride that keeps us from admitting we need His help. We often try to find a way to do this without God. I hope by now we realize that we not only can't, but shouldn't.

If you were drowning in a raging sea and someone came along to throw you a lifeline, would you say "no thanks I got this?" Here we have available to us on a daily basis, an *always ready, ever-present help. (Psalm 46:1)*

He's throwing you a lifeline. Take it. He will gently guide you into calmer waters.

In fact, let's be open to this scripture as wonderful news. We are about to be set free from pain and shame and guilt and fear. The past has had its day, and it's over. We can fight this fact or let it free us. We have a God who understands how hard it is to let go, and will provide us the graces we need. Let's turn to Him now with a willingness to be made new, to be a person fully alive in the present and hopeful about our future.

Maybe for some of us, "the past" is obvious. There may be a specific experience in our lives that we know still needs healing. Some of our experiences may have even been very serious or life threatening. Some of us may be frozen in time with the pain of grief and loss. Some of us may be suffering from an addiction of some kind. Some of our past experiences may involve committing terrible offenses toward others and causing grief or pain to come into someone else's life and we can't forgive ourselves for it. Or maybe for others of us it's more subtle.

Maybe there's just a feeling of uneasiness we can't put our finger on. We get hurt easily, and we don't know why. Maybe there's a lot of anger within us that we've become aware of, but we don't know where it comes from. Perhaps there's a childhood wound we have carried over into our adulthood. Things on the surface may look fine, but we know something is lacking. We don't have inner peace.

We won't compare experiences here. We will just focus on this fact - we are all wounded in some way and God wants to heal us. Something in our heart is unfinished and needs spiritual attention. We have a God who desires to set us free and He's up for the job. All we have to do is let Him, really let Him. Give Him permission to come into your life in a new way. He's knocking at the door of your heart. Let Him in.

Reflection

Am I willing to accept that the past is over?

How often do I recall to memory the pain of the past?

Am I in charge of my thoughts or are my thoughts in charge of me?

Am I in need of God's healing touch in my life or do I think I can handle things on my own?

Do I believe God Loves me or am I still angry with Him for allowing this to happen?

Am I willing to have a future that is different than the one I planned on?

Prayer

Dear Lord, your instruction here is clear. To no longer remember the past and that you desire to do something new with my life. It couldn't be clearer. This is exactly what I want too but I find it hard. I'm so used to living this way. I recognize I need to let go, to move forward, but I need Your help. I know You have a plan for me, a better one, a right one and I'm asking now for the grace to be open to it. You are more powerful than my past and can bring me the healing I need. I ask you to heal all painful memories, hurtful words, broken relationships, regrets, mistakes, guilt, shame, anything that still has a hold on me and prevents me from fully living and enjoying the present moment. Amen.

22

Chapter 2

"I am the Lord your God... You shall have no other gods before me."

~ Exodus 20:2-3

What does this have to do with letting go of the past and being made new? Everything! Too often we put things, situations and even other people ahead of God. We find the past hard to let go of because we become attached to these things, things that should never have been given so much power over our lives to begin with.

God tells us here, that He alone is God and there is no other. This is so important that He makes it the first of all the commandments, so we should probably pay attention to it. He's not saying it harshly or with condemnation and He's not saying it for His benefit. It's for our own joy that He tells us this. Hear Him say it gently, simply stating a fact that He knows will be important for us to understand.

We see a good God guiding us and instructing us already. God wants us to be at peace. God wants us to be happy, so He knows we first need to learn the natural order of things. God came first. We came second.

This is the first thing He wants us to know because everything else is based upon it. Our lives stem from this fact. He's the Creator. We're not.

The world tells us the opposite - that we can make God into whatever we want Him to be, that He's up for grabs. It teaches us that whatever suits us is just fine and that God should accommodate us. That God is whatever we think He is and I'm sure we think Him up to be someone who coincidentally is in line with our likes and dislikes. But that would make *us* the Creator. We would then be creating God. We would be creating Him into *our* image and likeness instead of the reverse.

Think about it, if God were whoever everyone wanted Him to be, there would be many gods, not one. There would probably be one god for each of us. So God makes it clear from the get go that there's just one God and it's Him. This lays the foundation for everything else in life.

God does more than just send a message in this commandment, He's also showing us that He wants to communicate with His people and reveal Himself to us. He wants us to know who He is and what sort of life we should lead.

To some the commandments sound restrictive, as if having rules holds us back. It's quite the opposite. The commandments set us free. They reveal a loving God who instructs His children and leads them in the right direction, one that will take them to eternal happiness. Not only do we know what way is the right way, we also know that we have a God who will guide us and help us. He wants to talk with us, to have relationship with us. This is still true today.

We hold onto our past when we fear the future. If we really understood that we have a bright future ahead of us that is not dependent on our circumstances, we would have peace. If we believed that God has a great plan for our lives that will last forever, we would have hope.

If we understood that we are not wasting time here, but using it wisely in prayer and growing in our relationship with God, we would have purpose. If we could only grasp that we were made for heaven, to spend eternity with God, we would easily turn to His Mercy and not despair because of our sins. If we accepted that God lives inside of us, and therefore is always with us no matter where we go, we would be happy.

Yes, happy! Because the happiness we seek can only be found in God's Love, something we already have within us. We just need to stop pushing Him away and let Him into our lives. We need to pray, and ask Him for the grace to accept His Love for us when we feel so unlovable. We need to understand that when Jesus spoke, He was speaking to all of us! He Loves us. Yes, a new life is waiting for us, wherever we are.

If we truly understood that God's plan is perfect, we wouldn't fear the future, we wouldn't fear anything. But we're human and we do. God wants to relieve our fears and bring us peace.

So it's not our place to decide who God is. It's our place to *discover* who He is. It's our job to seek Him out and let Him reveal Himself to us, something we see from the commandments that He already desires to do. When we

25

put God in second place, third place, last place or even no place, we don't experience the fullness of His Love and His inner voice guiding our steps. This scripture tells us He belongs in first place.

<u>Reflection</u>

Do I see God's commandments as harsh and mean, or as loving instruction to guide me?

What or who have I made into a god?

Am I willing to accept God's rules for my life or do I think I should make all the rules?

Do I even believe I have a future?

Can I see that God lives within me or do I think He's far away?

Am I willing to put God first in my life?

Prayer

Dear Lord, You alone are God. I thank you for revealing Yourself to humanity over and over again. But I long to know you myself, personally. I've created an image of You in my mind that may or may not be true but I desire to know what You're really like. My heart tells me You're real and that You love me. But I want more. I want to believe it, I want to know it. I believe You still speak to us today. Help me to take time to listen for you. Help me to turn to You in prayer, in some quiet time. Help me to turn off the noise that prevents me from hearing the stirrings of my heart, the voice of my God. I ask for Your help, Your grace to start this process of getting to know You better. Amen.

Chapter 3

So whoever is in Christ is a new creation: the old things have passed away; behold, new things have come.

2 Corinthians 5:17

Isn't this what we want? To be made new? To be refreshed, and light in heart, mind and spirit? We want to let go of the old heaviness in our hearts and be set free with the hope of new things to come. God tells us here that we can be completely transformed and made brand new!

Sometimes we think things will never change. It's easy to be tricked into thinking there is nothing more, nothing better, that the past is here to stay. But we must focus on what God tells us and He tells us here that new things are on the way.

This scripture is more than just positive thinking. This is a valuable teaching. We are made new *"in Christ."* In other words, not in something else. We look in many places for this new beginning we want. We hope to find a new job or a new relationship that will bring us fulfillment. We think maybe if we move or change our environment, things will get better. The thing is, we take ourselves with us wherever we go. If we don't have inner peace in our current circumstances there is no guarantee that we will have it in a new circumstance. There are certainly times when these things are good and the Lord is calling us to

29

make these changes in our lives, but the change we seek *within* us will not be realized from outside of us.

Jesus makes all things new! Until we accept that He is the answer, we will have a very difficult time trying to make a new start. *"In Christ"* we are brought to new life! We are not made new by looking at Christ or talking about Christ or even thinking about Christ. We are made new by *living in Christ*. Jesus lives in our heart and calls us to live in His. He has a love for us that is beyond our imagination and as we grow in this love, we will change.

God wants us to believe in His Goodness. He knows the past has a hold on us and that we need His help to be set free from it. We must focus our thoughts on the here and now and in the bright future ahead.

God works in us when we are *open* to Him working in us. If we close God off and cut Him out of our lives how can He help? He would be an unwelcome guest forcing Himself on us and He doesn't do that. In order to let *the old things pass away* we must be open to the new things coming and this only happens through faith.

Faith during trying times is not a simplistic idea to help you get through. It's an actual weapon against despair. Faith is powerful. It sets God in motion and fills us with hope. Faith is a gift God wants to give us that we must practice and develop. We must ask for this gift and be open to receiving it.

It's difficult to believe in something we can't see or understand. It's hard to even understand why God would work this way. The world runs on intellect (most of the time) and God works by faith. You can spend your life trying to figure out why or give it a try.

He tells us to believe in the good news, that we can be a *new creation*, that the old things can pass away and we can be created again in heart and spirit, free and better than ever! If this is something you've not believed before, be willing to believe it now. Ask God for the grace to believe this, that the past can truly be forgotten, that there's reason to hope. This scripture encourages us to let go of the old completely, to become a new person, and a happier one.

Reflection

How do I feel when I think about a "new me"? What do I picture?

Is my heart heavy? What weighs it down?

How much energy does it take to carry my past around with me all day?

Am I willing to let "new things" come into my life?

Is my faith strong or have I lost some of it?

Am I willing to allow God to work in my life?

<u>Prayer</u>

Dear Lord, I need to let the old pass away. The past serves no purpose for me anymore. It's empty. It's not even there because it no longer exists and yet I am attached to it. I am holding onto it. I want to be where You are and You are not in the past. I have become so used to seeing my life in retrospect but now I want to begin seeing a bright future ahead. It's never too late to be inspired, to be enthused, to be hopeful, to be given a new idea or a new dream, and I ask you to give me one. You are My God and I want to live in Your Love for me and Trust Your perfect plan for my life, which is superior to mine. Please help me to begin a new way of living and believing in the good things, the amazing things You have in store for me. Amen.

Chapter 4

*For I know well the plans I have in mind for you, declares
the Lord, plans for peace and not disaster, plans to give
you a future full of Hope.*

~ Jeremiah 29:11

Sometimes our plans fall through. Maybe it feels like a disaster. Especially when our hopes were high ones, it can feel like a tragedy occurred in our lives when things don't work out like we planned. We pray and we try, and when things don't work out we naturally get discouraged or even lose faith. Maybe we don't try anymore, afraid we'll just be let down again. All of this creates an unrest in our souls that keeps us stuck in the past instead of looking forward.

The Lord reminds us here that unlike our plans, His plans both work and bring us peace. Not a false peace that the world tries to give us, but an inner peace that can't be explained, that only be found in Jesus. *"Peace I leave with you. My peace I give you. I do not give to you as the world gives. Do not let your hearts be troubled and do not be afraid." (John 14:27)* God's plans for us are peace. The peace that will satisfy our souls can only be found in Christ. Yet, we search for this peace everywhere else. Well, why not try something new?

When our plans fall through, we may feel that God isn't there and that He doesn't care. Sometimes it feels like God is just watching our plans fall apart without any interest in what's going on in our lives. We feel alone and abandoned. It's easy to feel this way when life gets hard. God understands our human nature and our weaknesses. He knows we get disappointed in Him sometimes, but He tells us here that it's only because He has a *better* plan than we did. In humility we need to accept that God has a wider view of things. He can assess the situation more clearly. He sees the whole picture. We only see our part.

This is why it's important to remind ourselves what scripture teaches us. His plans for us are not for tragedy or failure. He wants us to have a *"future full of hope."* This might be hard to believe, especially if you're not in a hopeful kind of place right now. So let's pray for the grace to believe this, asking God to increase our faith at times like these. Let it be enough for now to believe that God hears our prayers and He *wants* the best for us. He's a Good God! He's not just sitting back passively watching you suffer. Soon you will see that He's active in your life and carrying you to a better place.

We have a future! We can continue to struggle to have the future that we planned on, or we can save ourselves a lot of pain and ask God to reveal His. His plans *always* work out! But only if we are open to them. He won't force us to choose Him. He wants us to come to Him freely and ask Him for another way - *His* way!

This is probably one of the most refreshing scriptures in the Bible and we should be encouraged to read it often. It helps to be reminded that God, first of all, has a plan for our lives, and secondly that it's a good one. His plan is right. His plan is best. His plan is perfect. It's the one that will fulfill us and keep us encouraged.

Remember, God wants to make us Happy with a capital "H". A little "h" is not enough for Him. He wants us to have everything. We think we know what will make us Happy, but God actually does. He asks us repeatedly to trust Him, to have faith in Him, to allow Him to work in our lives. When we let go and let Him in, we will then see His wonderful plan unfold.

Reflection

What's the plan for my life? Do I have one?

Have I been holding on to this plan too tightly? Trying to control its outcome?

What has happened in the past that caused me to be disappointed in God or doubt His Goodness?

Am I disappointed with myself?

Can I see that God Loves Me and that He is active in my life, even when I don't understand what's happening?

Is it possible that His plans could be better than mine?

Am I willing to give my plans over to God?

<u>Prayer</u>

Dear Lord, You know how often my plans have failed. Even those that I thought were part of Your Will for me. Please turn my confusion into hope, my tears into joy, my pain into Holiness, and give me a sincere desire to do what You want and be open to the new and wonderful life you have waiting for me.

It's hard to picture what lies ahead but I only need to know that You will lead me there and be with me wherever I go. Your plans are the right ones for me and I ask for the grace to stop insisting on my way, and to trust Yours. Help me to never fear Your plan for my life, to Trust that Your Will is what will make me Happy, that you are a God of Love and Joy and want to give me something wonderful. Amen.

Chapter 5

I will give you a new heart,

and put a new spirit in you.

~ Ezekiel 36:26

A brand new heart, a heart washed clean of the past and the pain. A heart made new in the Love of God, is what our souls crave.

Our hearts belong to God. He created them. They are His. We don't tend to look at it that way. We think it's our own and so we try to heal it ourselves. The truth is that our Creator created the human heart. He knows it well, and understands it better. He wants to renew it and, unlike us, He knows how to.

God knows our old heart is a heavy one. He knows what weighs it down. Maybe we don't talk about it much with others but God knows every detail. He knows what wounds are still there. Maybe there are things we're not even aware of that God knows needs healing.

When we turn to God in prayer, and give Him our heart, He can wash clean those wounds with His healing Love. He knows how fragile our hearts are. He's not going to rip the wound open. He will be gentle. He's the one who knows what our hearts really need. He asks for our entire heart, not some of it. He wants our whole heart, so He that He can make our heart whole.

Everyone needs a heart renewal. Every day we need to surrender our hearts to the Sacred Heart of Jesus for a good cleaning. It doesn't take long to let old grudges come back, to let unforgiveness in, to take back an area of our life that we really don't trust God with. So for this reason we must turn our heart to God regularly until it becomes a habit.

God wants to give us a new heart and a new spirit. If our spirit has been broken then there's no energy, no hope, there's instead despair and darkness. God is a God of new beginnings, of light, of enthusiasm. He not only wants to heal us but He wants to energize us to bring His healing love to others as well.

Reflection

What is my idea of a *new* heart?

Am I willing to surrender my heart to the One who made my heart?

How often do I pray? Do I talk to God about the things that have wounded me?

Can I admit that my heart needs God's healing touch?

Why do I hesitate to give God my heart?

Prayer

Dear Lord, only You know the condition of my heart. Even those close to me could never know what You do. Therefore, I come confidently to You who understands, to give me a new heart and a new spirit, one that is light and bright, free and clean, hopeful and happy.

At all times I need this freshness of heart and I ask for it now. Help me to unload my burdens to You, to Trust in Your Love for me. Help me to cast my cares upon You, for you care for me. Help me to be willing to let go of this old heart of mine and allow you to take all of it into your healing hands. My prayer is a big one Lord. I ask you for a new heart, a new spirit, and a new life free from the burden and pain of my past. Amen.

Chapter 6

The favors of the Lord are not exhausted, His mercies are not spent. They are renewed each morning, so great is His faithfulness.

~ Lamentations 3:22-23

Ever think there is a limit to how much God will help you? That there is only so much to go around? This scripture reminds us of God's abundant love. God's Mercy never runs out. God never gets tired of pouring out blessings on us. There is no end to His goodness. He has no limit.

His Mercy is *"renewed each morning"*. This means we can start over, at any time, every day. This is the purpose of this book, to encourage one another to begin again in a new way, now, today, bringing ourselves and our broken past to Jesus to heal us. Knowing perfectly well that we will need Him to heal us again tomorrow and the next day and the next day.

This scripture teaches us that every day God is merciful. We can start again, at any moment. God asks us to be faithful to Him and we are reminded here that He is faithful to us. He doesn't care what our past was, He just cares that we come back. He wants us to come to Him, to trust Him again and start over with a clean slate.

Life is full of new beginnings. Each moment is an opportunity to live a new life. I can be a better person than I was five minutes ago and if I mess up I know Jesus will be there for me five minutes from now. Chances are I will need Him again five minutes after that. It's so refreshing to hear that we can start over fresh each day.

We are human. We are constantly making mistakes and saying and doing things we wish we could take back. We have many faults but we also have a God who loves us unconditionally. This isn't easy to understand in a world that demands a price be paid for our actions. We, as Christians understand that the price has already been paid on the Cross, and the gift that Jesus gives us of His Love and Mercy are free!

Let's have the humility to turn to our faithful God and allow Him to pour out His Mercy upon us. God will never grow tired of loving us and if we let Him, He will transform our lives.

Reflection

Do I believe that I should only pray for *certain things*?

Do I think there are only so many mistakes I'm allowed to make? A limit I can't exceed?

Do I expect perfection from myself?

Does it feel like there is only so many times God will forgive me before He stops?

Prayer

Dear Lord, I understand now that I am always in Your heart and you're always thinking of me. You are always by my side helping me and loving me, yet so often I fail to see you there because I am so busy about other things. I pass right over you trying to do it all myself. I am truly sorry for not paying more attention to you and I ask for the grace to recognize Your presence in my life and to begin to trust You completely. This alone would be a big change for me as trust is not my specialty. Too many times in life people don't give us a second chance and we can easily begin to think that You wouldn't either. Clear this confusion and help me to understand that you give me chance after chance and will never grow tired of it. I want to be made new. I am in need of Your great Love and Mercy. Help me to put my pride aside and permanently place myself in Your care and compassion. Amen.

Chapter 7

*If you don't like something change it; if you can't change
it, change the way you think about it.*

~ *Mary Engelbreit*

We can't change everything. However, we don't have to keep thinking about things the same way. We can accept our limitations, realizing we're not perfect and neither is anybody else.

The past can't be changed. We can't go back. We can only move forward or stay stuck. Thinking about the past is part of the problem, so changing the way we think about it is part of the solution. We can take another look at it, from another angle, and define it again.

As we adjust the lens, it won't appear so big anymore. We will realize we have been giving the situation much more power than it deserves and we can then put it back in its proper place - the past - not our present! We can give God first place in our lives instead, and place the situation in His capable hands.

Let's never underestimate the power of prayer. When it feels like we will stay stuck forever, let's turn to our Lord and speak to Him as the gentle friend that He is. Prayer is a powerful tool in the face of needed change. The answer may not come as we want, but it will come. God will bring His healing Love into this situation but in a way that is best for us and all involved. The situation may still be there but it will no longer be the end of the world. It will have lost its power. We will have turned it over to the One who has power over it.

Let's ask God to shine His light on the situation and make it new. Things will begin to look differently as we give it to God. This is a habit worth forming and a grace from God worth asking Him for. Through prayer and His guidance we will be quick to take a second look at what's happening in our lives and determine if there's a better way to approach things.

As we look to the future we will have to adopt a new vision. We're still in the early stages of surrender but as we learn to let go of the past in our hearts, we must let go of it in our minds as well.

We are so used to thinking a certain way, and now that way doesn't help us anymore. It's time for a *new way*. Something different has to happen in order for something different to happen and this is where we can start - through prayer and a new attitude.

God knows it's not easy to accept a difficult situation. He's here with us on this journey as we try to figure things out, and unlike us, He has the answer. He *is* the answer. Let's turn to Him for guidance and inspiration, to enlighten our mind, to shine His light in our life and help us to see things more clearly.

Reflection

How do I see this situation? Am I willing to see it differently?

Do I accept my limitations or do I expect perfection?

Have I ever even asked God to shine His Light on this situation so that I may see it differently?

How long am I willing to go on thinking about things the way I always have been?

Prayer

Dear Lord, you know every detail of this situation I bring to You now. You know how much of it is in my control and how much is not. Please give me a new way of seeing this. Help me to surrender the matter to you. Help me to change the way I look at it. I ask you to grant me the graces I need to see this in a new light, Your Light and to be set free from all worry, sadness or fear. I ask for this grace for myself, and for others, who naturally see things from their own perspective as well. Give us Your Heavenly perspective and a new outlook on life so that we may live in the New Way you want us to. Amen.

Chapter 8

*Do not conform yourselves to the standards of this world,
but let God transform you inwardly, by a complete change
of your mind....*

~ Romans 12:2

The change we're seeking is huge. We're reading this book because our old way of doing things hasn't brought us the fulfillment we hoped for and we know there must be something more to life than what we've experienced so far.

The world makes it easy for us to stay as we are, without challenging us to become better people. It teaches us to be as comfortable as possible with as little effort as possible, while making ourselves the creators of our own eternal happiness. God tells us here to reject that.

What the world forgets to teach us is that there is a spiritual law to be obeyed, that God comes first. The world says *our will* should come first. This is more likely to lead us away from God and so God tells us here not to conform ourselves to the world's standards, because these standards are set pretty low and can take us down the wrong path, away from Him.

This scripture tells us that what we need is an overhaul of our old self, to be utterly transformed, to undergo a *complete change* of our mind, not just a little bit, but to be made brand new.

How does this transformation take place? From the inside out! Let's listen to this scripture again. *"Let God transform you inwardly ..."* So what do we do? We pray. We ask God for the grace to surrender our lives to Him completely. We open our hearts to the action of The Holy Spirit, who is Love itself. We *seek first the kingdom of God,* and everything else falls into place.

We stop trying to earn our way, fight our way, or keep our way. We stop trying to be right and we start trying to forgive. We accept that apart from God, on our own, we are nothing. But we also accept that we are not on our own! We have a God who is with us, every step of the way. He doesn't leave our side not even for a second. He Loves us like no other, and we mean everything to Him.

We need God and God knows what we need. He can bring about the change within us that we want. Through prayer, God will help and heal and set our hearts free - but we have to ask for this. This may not come easily for those of us who like to solve our own problems, on our own. Why do we have such a hard time asking for help?

Pride is the culprit here. It's the culprit in opposition to any personal or spiritual growth. Pride says we can do it by ourselves. We don't need God and we certainly won't admit our *dependence* upon God. Many find this a difficult word, but really, dependence on anything other than God would make it a difficult word. We are dependent upon God for our very next breath. Our hearts do not beat because we tell them to. There is a life source sustaining us at every moment. This life source has a name, and He loves you.

With an understanding that we are not alone, that there is a loving God by our side, we can embark upon the journey of changing ourselves with confidence. We can be assured that we will receive grace because scripture has shown that our Creator wants this more than we do.

God wants inner peace for us all, to heal us and make us whole. He wants us to continually improve ourselves, to mature and develop spiritually because He knows where it will lead - to Him. So we can be certain He will help us get there.

Reflection

In what way have I allowed the world, or things, or even people, to get in the way of my relationship with God?

What standards do I set for myself?

Have I been trying to make changes on the outside in order to achieve peace on the inside?

Am I comfortable asking for help?

Do I feel I need to solve my problems on my own?

Do I see how interconnected we all are, that we need God but we also need one another?

51

<u>Prayer</u>

Dear Lord, so many times I have tried to change. I no longer want to try without You. With You by my side I can overcome any fault I have, anything that needs improvement. I want to better myself. I want to be free of the anxieties of life and cope better with situations that are difficult. I ask You humbly now, to grant me a New Way of approaching change since my way doesn't work as well as I'd like. Grant me the grace to embrace the Love you offer me.

You are real. You are with me. I am dependent upon You and that's a great place to be. I wouldn't want to be dependent upon anyone or anything else. Who better than Love itself to show me the Way. Please help me in what I know will be a daily struggle to let go of my pride, let others into my life, and let Your love into my heart. Please pour out your grace upon me. Amen.

Chapter 9

Consider how hard it is to change yourself and you'll understand what little chance you have in trying to change others.

~ Jacob M. Braude

Trying to be a better person is worth it. Becoming one is not easy. There is so much resistance to change. We know what we have to do, whether it's eat better, exercise more, forgive more easily, be more positive, etc. Yet we don't do it. We fail at our attempts to improve ourselves but have extremely high expectations for others to.

It's easier to look at someone else's life than to look at our own. We can see the changes everyone else needs to make in their lives, which are often the same ones we need to make in ours, and we just can't understand why they don't make them. Then we get disappointed or even angry with them for not doing what they should be doing.

We are not fit to judge anyone else's circumstances. Our view is limited. We can only see from the outside in and the same is true for them. Others can't see what's within us either. They can't see what we've experienced, our childhoods, our hopes and dreams, our anxieties, our fears of the future, what we think or how we feel - all of which impact our decisions today.

Only God sees this far into the human heart. We have a God who loves us unconditionally, who understands how hard change is. He wants to help us become the people we were created to be. When we grasp how complicated we are, what makes us think that others aren't as complicated with their own issues. We therefore, are not fit to judge or attempt to change them.

"How can you say to your brother, 'Brother, let me take the speck out of your eye,' when you yourself fail to see the plank in your own eye? You hypocrite, first take the plank out of your eye, and then you will see clearly to remove the speck from your brother's eye." (Luke 6:42)

We are all guilty of judging others, but doing so doesn't change us one bit. We are not called to live someone else's path, we are called to live our own. We are called to live God's plan for *our* lives and should concern ourselves with that.

Of course we should be supportive of others and available to them in providing guidance in a prayerful way, if they seek out our advice, but most of the time they don't. Most of the time we are forcing our own judgmental opinions on others without their request or consent. Even worse, we may do so behind their back when they are not able to defend themselves or the situation they're in.

Often times, our intentions are good and our opinions are well thought out with the other person's best interest at heart. But who are we to drop our opinions into their life when we have our own to live. Only God knows the whole story. Let's pray for them and allow God to work His healing grace in their lives as we pray for Him to do the same in ours. Let's place our opinions of others into God's hands and ask Him to help us bring out the best in people.

When we get frustrated with others or discouraged in our own efforts, let's remember that we can choose what we do and say regardless of how we feel or think. We can choose to be patient with others, to give them room to be human when they make mistakes, and be supportive of their life's situation as they go through hard times too.

We must also treat ourselves with the same interior respect. We have to be careful not to judge ourselves too harshly and not expect perfection. We try, and we fail, and we try again. This is the human condition, and we are part of it.

Above all, the number one reason we shouldn't judge others is because Jesus has commanded us not to. That alone is reason enough. He knows our humanity and He knows how very often we fail to obey this command, but through His Mercy we can continue to improve in this area of our lives and become people of good intentions, ready to encourage, stick up for, and think the best of others, rather than the worst.

God Loves us, and He Loves those we judge also. We may think we have a right to expect others to change, but we don't have any "rights" over another human person ever. It is possible however, that once we change ourselves we will see people and situations in a better light as judgments leave our life, and Christ enters into it.

We all have a place in our hearts that only God can touch and change begins there. These are areas that need healing. Everyone has them. When we invite God into our hearts with His Healing Love, we change. Too often we make change more complicated than it has to be. Most often, change will occur with a new awareness of God's Love. Things are always seen more clearly in The Light of Christ.

There's no way around it, personal growth is hard work, and at times painful. Change doesn't come easy but it doesn't have to. God has equipped us with the tools we need to do what's difficult. With His grace supporting us, we can be less judgmental of others and more forgiving to those who judge us.

Reflection

When was the last time I judged someone?

When was the last time I spread gossip?

When I form an opinion of someone, do I present it to others as the truth, or as my opinion?

How much of what I say about other people is actually necessary?

How often to I try to improve myself?

How often do I try to improve others?

What would happen if I minded my own business and doubled my efforts to live my own life better?

Prayer

Dear Lord, too often I criticize what others do. I so easily find fault in others, yet fail to see my own. It's easier for me to look at them than to take a good look at myself. I have made a habit out of judging others and I want to stop. Help me to look within and recognize the changes I need to make in my own life. Help me to recognize what I have control over and what I don't. Help me to leave the changes others need to make in their lives in Your hands, not mine. Through Your eyes, help me to look upon others in a much kinder light. Thank you for your unending patience with me and my faults and please help me to be patient with others. Please grant me the gift of humility, to be gentle with others and also with myself and to start living in this new way, today. Amen.

Chapter 10

If you're in a bad situation, don't worry it'll change. If you're in a good situation, don't worry it'll change.

~ John A. Simone, Sr.

Nothing stays the same. Life is constantly changing. People change, circumstances change. When we are in the moment of suffering it feels like nothing will ever be different than what we are experiencing right then. We think it will be this way forever. When we are in a bad situation our vision is limited. When we are in a good situation, the same is true. It will change. We think in that moment also that everything will stay wonderful.

There is only one thing in this world that doesn't change and that is God. He doesn't change because He always is. He is in a state of "is" called the present moment. He is the great "*I AM*", *the Alpha and the Omega - the beginning and the end.* He is one God, all the time, because for Him there is no such thing as time. He is the same at every moment of our lives. In Hebrews 13:8 it says "*Jesus Christ is the same yesterday, today, and forever.*"

In regard to letting go of the past, there is value in this moment right now. We may feel our choices are between the pain of the past (which is out of our control) and fear of the future, (which is out of our control.) This is a very frustrating and unhealthy way to live. There is, however, another choice called the present moment. This is the

59

moment where God is and when we align ourselves with where He is, everything falls into place and we find the freedom we are looking for.

Sometimes it feels like the present moment is hard to find. We have so much on our minds and on our hearts. Our thoughts take us everywhere but here in the now. Especially the concern for the next moment. That alone robs us of peace. Think about how often we focus on what we are about to do next rather than what we are doing now. The present moment is here, whether we ignore it or not. When we embrace the present moment, new things reveal themselves.

We cannot change God. We cannot change others. We can only change ourselves. So rather than try to fight time, let's try to embrace it and grow emotionally and spiritually from it. Growing into a deeper relationship with our unchanging God is what the present moment brings us. It's comforting to know that He is with us in both the good times and bad times of our lives, both of which will change ... and change again.

God is our rock. He is a steady, faithful, reliable friend who never leaves, who never changes, and accepts us as we are. That doesn't mean He wishes us to stay as we are. We are called to change. We are called to a *new* life in Christ.

Let's ask God for a new way to approach the changes that take place in our lives. Let's ask for a new outlook and be open to a new life, embracing all God wants to give us, as we live in the present moment.

Reflection

What do I wish would change?

Are these changes under my control?

In what way does my life feel out of control?

Do I see God as a stable and solid rock in my life or do I see God as changing from day to day?

How many moments do I waste thinking about other moments?

Am I willing to start making better use of the time God has given me?

Am I willing to turn to God in prayer for a moment - this moment - the present one - the one He lives in - and listen for His voice in my heart?

Prayer

Dear Lord, in a world that is filled with such uncertainty and empty promises, where things change from one day to the next, from one hour to the next, You alone are reliable. You alone are unchanging and always present. We can always count on You. You are good, all the time. You never leave us on our own. Help me to see that. Help me to truly believe in Your presence in my life and no longer feel your absence. Help me to stop trying to change You and instead start trying to change me. Help me to look to You, not as a last resort, but as my first choice, in all things.

Please teach me how to pray to You. Show me what it is that I need to change first, what I need to change most. Help me to start where You want me to. Please help me to change my own behavior so that I may live as You desire. Help me to be less concerned with the changes others are making, or not making, in their lives and simply do my best to improve my own. Dear Lord, help me not to fear change because I know that no matter what happens, You will always be there with me. Amen.

Chapter 11

I came so that they might have life

and have it more abundantly.

~ John 10:10

We don't have a small God. Our God is one of abundance. It's very popular to think this means He will help you get lots of money and a big house but let's explore what this abundant life He desires entails.

What is most lacking in the world? In my opinion it's love. The world has its own version of what love is and we use the word interchangeably in many situations, such as describing the affection we have toward our loved ones and in describing our taste for pizza. Who doesn't love pizza but the point is the word *love* has so many different levels of its meaning.

It's a word that holds its highest level of meaning in the person of Jesus Christ, the Son of God. God is Love. Jesus is God. If we really want to know what true love is all about, we have to look at Jesus and the life He lived.

Jesus came into this world to set us free. As stated here in this scripture, to give us *life*. This life he refers to is not our existence, it's how we live it, it's who we are. It's what we can be. It's what He wants us to be and it's not limited, it's abundant.

This life He wants us to have is His own. It's a life in His Spirit. It's a Love the world and everyone in it, can't give us, only He can. Accepting that it's time to stop expecting others to be like a god when we already have one is the first big step toward receiving it.

Let's stop living as if we have such a tiny God who can only handle so much or He will have a nervous breakdown. God is bigger than any problem you can throw at Him. He is bigger than anything and the Creator of everything. He can handle it. He can move mountains. Let's take what He's giving us and live an abundant life of love.

Let's allow Jesus to give us the life He suffered and died to give us. A life filled with His Holy Spirit, a life that glorifies our Heavenly Father, a life that brings us joy, and motivates us to bring that joy to others.

Reflection

What does the word *Love* mean to me?

Do I attribute the same value of this word to God as I would toward other people and situations?

What does the phrase "abundant life" mean to me? Do I think of it in terms of spiritual gifts and graces from God?

Do I see God as limited, only willing to give so much?

Do I ever stop to really reflect on what Jesus has given me by giving me His *Life* on the cross?

Prayer

Dear Lord, I desire a more abundant life and I know you have both the power and desire to give it to me. Please take my old definition of what that means. Take all the things I thought would make me happy. I let go of them to You now. The life I now want is the one you want for me. Make this my heart's desire from now on. Help me to see that in serving you I receive this life. A life of joy and peace and satisfaction, overflowing with grace.

Please show me what this abundant life really means. This life You died to give me is full of everything my heart craves, help me not to ignore it any longer. You died so that I will live - forever! Help me to take a good look at my priorities and make sure You're at the top of the list. Please grant me the grace to accept a New Life in You! Amen.

Chapter 12

Eye has not seen and ear has not heard, and what has not entered the human heart, what God has prepared for those who love Him.

~ 1 Corinthians 2:9

There's something to look forward to. There's hope for the future. A future that is so wonderful it can't even be explained. Scripture tells us here we can't even picture it, that we've never even heard of anything so great, that those who love God will not be disappointed.

It sounds too good to be true. Perhaps if it came from somewhere else we could say it's an exaggeration but it comes from God. God gives us a little glimpse into how awesome His plans for us are. Of course He has a new life ready and waiting for us while here on earth, but His plans also include an eternal home in heaven, and it sounds like there's a lot to look forward too. This scripture doesn't describe any details about our future but declares clearly that it's gonna be good.

For now though, we are called to live in the world with this hope. Do you still have hope? Do you feel like giving up sometimes? You're not alone. We have all felt that way but each situation is different, and God knows yours. He knows what you've been through. He knows what you've hoped for. He knows it's hard. He is not indifferent to your life or what's going on in it. He is holding you in the palm of His hand, right now. He loves you and it pains Him to see you sad.

He wants you to know, through this scripture, that there's something more than what you've experienced so far. Something better. Both in this world and in the next, great things await you. He asks us to believe this and not to put our hope in things or people but *in Him*. He alone can give us the future that will bring us joy. We not only have hope but we have a reason to hope. We can stand firm on God's Word and trust that He will bring about what He says He will.

In a world that can be so despairing, hope is exactly what we need. In our hearts, where the deepest secrets between us and God reside, a light shines, and someday we will be able to see it.

Let's anticipate good things. Let's look forward to the surprises God has waiting for us. Let's also never forget, that God is within us and there is reason to be happy *now*, to hope now, while we wait for more good things to come. It's a matter of uncovering what is within us, finding God's voice and following it.

Reflection

When I think of my future, what do I see?

Does the pain of my past cloud the view of my future?

Is God in the picture?

Do I ever ask myself, "Is this it? Is this all there is?"

God made Heaven and earth on purpose with a Divine plan in mind, but do I feel like I'm a part of it?

Do I trust God with my future?

Prayer

Dear Lord, sometimes it's hard to believe that things will get better, that great things still await me. It's hard to picture my eternal home in Heaven when there is such despair here on earth. Please give me a new perspective. Help me to have faith, which is believing in what I can't see. May these words of Yours encourage me. Lord, you know how easy it is to get discouraged, to grow weary. It's hard to find the energy to try again. Sometimes it feels like this is all there is. That there's nothing more than what I've known or can imagine. But you tell me there's more and I believe You. Please grant me the grace to believe even more deeply in Your awesome plan for my life and grant me a New Way of hoping in You. Amen.

Chapter 13

Sing to the Lord, a New Song.

~ Psalm 96:1

The old song is easy, we know it by heart, we hear it every day. We may turn the volume up or down depending on certain factors but it's always playing in the background. It's not a very good song either. It's one that makes us feel badly about ourselves.

This one hit wonder keeps us stuck in the past. It has a lot of useless memories attached to it that no longer serve a purpose in our lives. This record keeps playing even when it's broken, and it sounds horrible. Mostly however, this song takes up too much air time. It doesn't make room for anything new or fresh or different. It just wants to hear the sound of its own voice and in the process, we become so accustomed to it that we forget it's there.

The lyrics are just as bad. With words like "I'm no good", or "no one loves me", or "nothing will ever change" you could see why it wouldn't be a big hit. Yet we bought it and we keep playing it. It's time to stop. Get rid of it. Return it. Put on something new.

God knows how wounded you are. He knows the reasons for this old song, what it meant to you, what it still means to you and why it still plays. But when we are wounded we don't always make the best decisions. When

71

we make poor decisions we don't always correct them as we should. When we don't correct them we allow them to become the norm and remain in their wrong state, sometimes for a long time. We live like a broken record spinning in circles, going nowhere. It's very important that we replace this record with something else. It's bringing us down and holding us back.

Let's pick a song with some lyrics that will uplift and inspire us! Let's pick something that will fill us with an appreciation for all we have. Let's ask God to help us find our voice in it all, and speak words of Life!

It isn't easy to change your tune. It might be one of the hardest things you'll do. Anytime you attempt to grow emotionally or spiritually you will have resistance. The past is strong. But our God is stronger.

Reflection

What's the song of my past playing in my head? What are the lyrics?

How does this song make me feel?

How long has this record been playing?

What can I replace it with?

Am I willing to change my tune and think new and more positive thoughts about my life? Or am I happy with the way things are?

Prayer

Dear Lord, I want to sing a new song. Yes, New. Can you believe that one Lord? Me, who for too long, has lived with this negative background noise. I've had enough of my old way of thinking. I want to replace it with something that is good, something that will build me up rather than tear me down. Something that will inspire me to be a better person and strive toward that goal every day. Something more positive than what I've been listening to in the past. I am responsible for allowing this tune to play for so long and I'm sorry I have. I need you to help me out of it. Help me to choose what I think about and choose what I say to myself over and over again. Please put a New song in my heart Lord, give me a New life and a New Spirit to sing it in. Make this my new normal and help me to keep the music going in the right direction. Amen.

Chapter 14

Every good gift and

every perfect gift is from above....

~ James 1:17

Thank you. These are two words that can mean so much to the one who hears them and can benefit even more the one who speaks them. Sometimes we are so caught up in our past and in our pain that we forget to be thankful for the good things we have.

When we have a spirit of thanksgiving in our prayers, we begin to see things a little differently. We realize God has been providing for us throughout our past, and will continue to provide for us in our future. A spirit of thanksgiving also lifts us up. It raises us to a new level of awareness of God's goodness, something that will counter feelings of depression and discouragement.

Too often we fail to thank God for the gifts He gives us. There are too many to even list here: the gift of life, the gift of our families and friends, the food we eat, the clothing we wear, the air we breathe, etc. It goes on and on. We can choose what we say to ourselves and we can make that decision today to thank God for His blessings each morning. We may not have all that we want, but we can try to be more appreciative of what we have.

We all need to do a better job of expressing our gratitude to God. It's easy to take things for granted. Often we forget how generous He is. Let's begin a *new way* of making gratitude a habit. Even when things are going badly we can find something to be thankful for, however small.

But there is another gift that we may or may not even think of thanking Him for, and that is the gift of Himself. God gives us His Spirit. The Holy Spirit is Love itself. The Holy Spirit and the gifts of the Spirit, such as wisdom, knowledge and faith, help us to grow in our spiritual life. In fact, these gifts allow us to *have* a spiritual life.

The Bible tells us that there are different gifts but the same Lord, which affirms that we are one body in Christ and have many parts. We are all connected, so everyone's gifts serve a purpose to build one another up. We are not supposed to hold onto our gift from God just for ourselves. All things from God are meant to be shared.

We all have something special to offer and as we see here in this scripture, *every good and perfect gift is from God.* So let's not only increase our gratitude for the gifts God gives us but let's also make an effort to better understand what they are, and discover which ones are uniquely ours.

All of God's gifts will bring blessings to others, so it is important that we find and develop our gifts so God can use us as He wishes. When we act on the gifts we have received, we fall into line with God's Will, and when we do, everything else straightens out.

Reflection

What am I grateful for?

When I pray, do I thank God or just ask Him for things?

Do I see God Himself as a Gift?

What am I good at? What are my spiritual gifts? Am I a good listener, do I take time out for others, do I pray?

What is it that I *want* to be good at?

Do I pray to God to give me special gifts, or to reveal His spiritual gifts to me, and to help me use these gifts?

How often throughout the day do I say *thank you*?

Prayer

Dear Lord, You know there are times when I feel like I have nothing left to give, nothing to offer. You also know how often I fail to recognize all that You have given me and to thank you as I should. I thank you now.

Thank you for every good and perfect gift you give to me and my loved ones. Thank you for being there for me through good times and bad, even when I fail to recognize it, I know by faith that You are there. Thank you for sending me Your Holy Spirit to strengthen me and guide me.

Lord, I feel that there is something special I can do, some purpose I have, some quality you have given me that you can use to serve others, but I'm not sure what it is. More often than not we see talent in others but fail to recognize it in ourselves. Please help me to see in me what You see in me, and to discover Your plan for my life, and follow it. Amen.

Chapter 15

Kind words are short and easy to speak,

but their echoes are truly endless.

~ Mother Teresa

Kind words are in short supply these days. We are all guilty of being wrapped up in ourselves sometimes or too busy to think of others. We all say hurtful and harmful things to one another on occasion.

Words matter. Once spoken, they can't be taken back, no matter how hard we try to or how much we apologize. It is so important to stop and think before speaking. To take the time to really listen to someone else's point of view, even if we disagree. After all, as we know, God gave us two ears and one mouth for a reason.

When we live in the past, we can easily overlook all that is going on in the present. We're not the only one with problems. We run the risk of becoming selfish and hurting others the way we were once hurt ourselves. We need to look up every now and then and make ourselves available to help others and be sensitive to what is going on in *their* lives. Speaking kind words is a great way to start!

Kindness is also a powerful weapon against cruelty because it comes from God. It is one of the fruits of the Holy Spirit (Galatians 5:22) Kindness is an act of Love and therefore holds greater power over things that go against love. Did you ever hear the phrase *"kill them with kindness"?* When we encounter people who are unkind to us, the temptation is to give it right back to them. But we are not called to do that. Jesus has told us, *"Love one another, as I have Loved you." (John 13:34)* He doesn't say treat others the way they treat us. We are told to follow *His* example. To love others, the way *He* loves us, not the way anybody else does. This is hard. But it's clear.

Kindness is not weakness, it's strength, especially when you are kind to someone when you don't feel like it. It takes a lot of strength to be nice to those who aren't nice to you. This is hardly weakness. We need to make the effort to practice this more, to make it more popular and since this is something God wants us to do we can also count on His grace to help us do it. God always gives us the graces we need to do His will.

There is something else that matters just as much ... the absence of kind words. Being so wrapped up in oneself that we don't even say anything at all. We don't even notice those around us who need a kind word spoken to them. We overlook those who are hurting. We think because we're ok, they're ok, and that may not be the case. A person may think they haven't said anything wrong, because they haven't said anything at all. But being overlooked or ignored can hurt also and we need to be mindful of it.

We must also remember to be kind to ourselves as well. This isn't always easy either. Sometimes it's harder. We're not perfect and we need to let go of any plans we have of being perfect. God loves us for who we are, not for what we do. Let's not think unkindly towards ourselves. Let's pay more attention to the things we think about and to the way we perceive ourselves. Let's change our attitude and our thoughts if they are negative and replace them with something healthy. We are children of God so let's treat ourselves accordingly.

Let's start fresh. Let's take all the unkind words we've spoken to others and all the unkind words ever spoken to us and throw them out the window and start over. Better yet, let's give them to God who will be happy to throw them away for us and give us a fresh start. While the spoken word cannot be taken back, we can still forgive - completely - by God's grace. This is when inner healing occurs and we are able to leave the past and move forward with our lives.

Bottom line, kind words can only do someone good and everyone needs them. They can make someone's day as much as hurtful words can harm someone's day. With God's help we can be people of profound kindness, always on the lookout for someone in need of it, and as a result find peace for ourselves too.

Reflection

Have I said anything kind to someone today?

Did I miss an opportunity to say something kind?

Do I know someone in my life right now going through a hard time? Am I willing to provide them a listening ear or a kind word?

Am I selfish? Do I only expect others to be kind to me?

Am I willing to look for occasions to be kind to someone rather than waiting for a situation to arise?

Who do I need to forgive? Who do I need to ask forgiveness from?

Prayer

Dear Lord, too often people don't take the time to speak words of kindness. In your great mercy, please bless those who hurt us and bless those who uplift us. Help us to recognize the importance and value of even the smallest acts of charity. Help us also to recognize Your voice in our lives. Help us to listen to our hearts in prayer to the kind words you wish to say to us today and grant us the graces we need to live a life of kindness toward others, and ourselves. Amen.

Chapter 16

Be still and know that I am God.

~ Psalm 46:10

Entering into silent prayer is the single most powerful tool we can use to develop our spiritual life. It is where we find God and in doing so, find us. Since we are made in His image, we will see ourselves reflected when we look at God. But first we have to look *for* Him.

We come to know God by spending time with Him. The invitation goes out to all, but not everyone responds. How pleased He must be when He sees us coming. Just the fact that we show up means He matters to us. We make time for what's important to us, and so if we enter into silent prayer, He must be important to us.

Of course we should use vocal prayers every day, read scripture, and talk with God about what's going on in our life. He is our greatest friend, and wants to be close to us. All prayer is good and pleasing to God. The purpose is to develop a relationship and that involves both talking and listening. In silent prayer, we listen.

In this type of prayer we don't use our time with words. We use our time by being still, by letting go of the noise in our life, inside and out, and being open to God's Love. We give God permission to love us just as we are. We don't pretend or try to be perfect. In humility we just come and *"be still."*

God is the *still small voice* within us and through quiet prayer we can hear His Heart speaking to our heart. This type of prayer involves letting go of everything, including our words. We trust that our Creator knows what is going on in our lives and we don't have to explain it to Him.

Through silent prayer, we find the present moment, the moment where God is. The moment is already there, we just need to remove the noise. This scripture encourages us to stay calm, to let go of worry, to have confidence and Trust in God. This is everything we seek, and we find it in stillness of our hearts. We will soon learn that God has always been there, and always will be.

When we enter into the quiet expect a lot of "stuff" to come to mind, old stuff, new stuff, good stuff, bad stuff. Let it go, let it just be. Release it and try to continue in prayer, surrendering everything into God's capable hands, and just continue to sit in the silence *with* Him.

This may take some getting used to at first. We are usually doing the talking in prayer, and here we are doing the listening. There will be resistance, as is the case any time we try to grow closer to God, so we should be prepared. There will be distractions, our mind will wander, we'll start to think of our to-do list for the day, etc. But let's try to stay focused on Christ, and make it a practice to faithfully give God a few minutes every day.

The Creator of time, deserves our time. Let's turn off the cell phone for a few minutes, turn off the T.V. and close our eyes and just sit with an open heart in the presence of God. It will change your life! It's simply a matter of whether you want to do it or not. Is this a priority for you?

The benefits of silent prayer are profound. Worries leave, answers come, and peace stills your soul. It takes patience and practice but it's worth it, and not to mention - God wants it. Repeatedly in scripture we hear God's desire to be close with His children. Silent prayer makes God happy. He desires to spend time with us too.

This scripture says so much in just one short sentence. Not only does it tell us to relax, stay calm, surrender and let go but it tells us what to do next. Be still and then what? "*Know that I Am God.*" Translation = Trust Me. God is telling us that He is taking care of everything. That we can leave it to Him, He can handle it.

He tells us not to worry, that He has everything under control. For those of us who live in the past, this is who we give it to. We surrender our past to One who can handle it. We give what is old to the One who can make it new. We give our past to the One who has a plan for our future. We Trust Him.

Trusting in God is not a thought or an idea, it's an action. Trusting Him to handle a situation better than we could is not passive. It's anything but, and it requires a great deal of humility, a letting go of our pride and our insistence that we should be able to do it ourselves without

Him. We can't do anything without God, not even take our next breath. We must admit we need Him. Let's Love Him too.

God gives us some deeply spiritual and practical advice here for our everyday life. *Be Still... and know that I Am God.* Let's enter into a quiet place in our heart and find the peace we've been looking for.

Reflection

Am I willing to spend time with God in quiet prayer?

What is it that I want to hear?

Do I trust God, or do I try to control Him?

Prayer

Dear Lord, you know my worries and how stressful life can be. I desire to spend some time each day with You in silence but something always comes up that stops me from being faithful to my time with You. I ask now for a special grace to come to you in the quiet and to be open to what you want to say to my heart. Help me to turn to You with all that's happening in my life, to have a heart to heart with You, and know that I can count on You. Please grant me a New Way of Trusting in Your Great Love and Mercy for me. Help me to make this a priority. While it's hard to find the time to pray and meditate each day, it's an even harder day if 1 don't. 1 know this place of silence will become my safe haven, where You will bring Love and Healing into my life. Amen.

Chapter 17

By prayer and petition, with thanksgiving, make your requests known to God.

~ Philippians 4:6

Rejoice in the Lord always. I will say it again: Rejoice! Let your gentleness be evident to all. The Lord is near. Do not be anxious about anything, but in every situation, by prayer and petition, with thanksgiving, present your requests to God. And the peace of God, which transcends all understanding, will guard your hearts and your minds in Christ Jesus. (Philippians 4:4-7)

We want a *New Way*. Our old way hasn't worked out for us. We want to be made new, to start fresh, to begin again, and it starts with prayer. Prayer is our connection to God. It's our telephone to His Heart. Sometimes we call God, and sometimes He calls us. But as long as we keep the lines of communication open and talk to Him regularly, we will find the answers we're looking for.

Maybe we think we have already given prayer a good try and didn't get anything out of it. The above scripture from Philippians might shine a new light on things. It's such a beautiful and practical verse, that teaches us how to approach prayer.

"Rejoice in the Lord always." How's that for starters? Rejoicing might be the last thing you feel like doing when

you are praying. Maybe you have a very serious request of God and you are in tears, how do you rejoice? It might sound like an unreasonable suggestion, but then we hear, "*I will say it again: Rejoice!*" Just in case we missed it the first time. It's not a mistake. We are called to rejoice when we pray.

Now, this doesn't mean we have to jump up and down and laugh and sing. It means we step out in faith knowing the end result - that everything is going to be ok. We praise God *in advance* of our prayer. We begin prayer by acknowledging His greatness, His faithfulness. This might take some practice, but God really is worthy of our praise. We might simply say, "Glory and Praise to you Almighty God." Even if we have to say it in tears.

Praise is powerful. It brings Light where there is darkness. It lifts our spirits and gives God His due Honor. It clears the way for our prayer and gives us reason to hope. We can be glad about this - that we have a God who we can talk to, a God who Loves us, who forgives us, who cares about us and who hears our prayers. That's something to rejoice over.

"Let your gentleness be evident to all". When we are a prayerful person, it should show. Others will be able to see that we have a relationship with the Lord, by our actions. We are reminded in this scripture that prayer is more than just words.

"The Lord is near. Do not be anxious about anything." God is in our hearts when we pray. We are not just praying *to* Him, we are also praying *with* Him. As we come to

know just how close God is to us, that He is always with us and never leaves us, our worries and fears will become less and less and we will begin to trust the Lord more and more.

"But in every situation, by prayer and petition, with thanksgiving, present your requests to God." God cares about it all! There is nothing too big or too small to come to God in prayer with. He wants our whole life, our whole heart, our whole mind.

He wants us to bring every situation to Him for healing. There's nothing going on in our lives that He doesn't care about. He wants to hear our petitions. We are called to ask and receive, and to do so with an appreciation for all the things we already have. When we pray with thanksgiving, we enhance our prayer and come before God with our requests as grateful children.

So what do we get from all this praying? *The peace of Christ.* Yes, we have our requests and petitions for ourselves and others, and God wants them. But more than anything else, prayer brings God's peace into our hearts during our trials.

This peace Jesus gives us is not like the peace the world tries to give us. His peace goes beyond our understanding, and it lasts forever. This peace will guard our hearts, keeping us safe and sound within, as we follow Christ. With this peace we can be "in the world but not of the world." It's a peace we can't buy, and we can't earn. It's Christ's free gift to us.

When we truly open our hearts to Jesus in prayer, and remain faithful to our prayer time each day, we will soon notice this peace within us, and so will others.

So let's revisit our prayer life once again. Let's praise God, believing He will help us. Let's make our requests with gratitude, knowing we are guarded by His peace within us.

Reflection

How do I currently pray?

Is praise or thanksgiving part of my prayer?

Do I trust God when I pray?

Do I believe God is close to me, and will hear my prayer? Or does it feel like He's far away, ignoring my voice?

Am I willing to give God access to every area of my life? Or only certain things?

What prayer of mine feels forgotten or still unanswered?

Am I willing to talk to God about what it meant to me?

Do I need to adopt a new attitude toward prayer?

Prayer

Dear Lord, I thank you for being with me each and every time I pray. There is no one like you Lord. You are worthy to be praised! Yet I barely mention this to you in prayer. I want you to know how grateful I am for all the blessings you have given me that I have failed to notice in the past.

Lord, You know how easily I get discouraged when I feel like you don't answer my prayers. Sometimes it feels like you don't really care, or that only certain things are important enough to pray for. You know how often I ask for things in prayer, how often I try to show You what I need or explain to You what I want, when You already know it. If I don't see the results I want, I give up too quickly. I realize now that I need an entirely New Way of praying.

Help me to be honest and open with You in prayer. Help me to let down my guard with you so that Your peace will come and guard me. Help me to confide in you as the friend you truly are. Help me to come to you with everything on my heart and mind, with all of my concerns for myself and my loved ones. Help me to pray constantly throughout the day with you, in mind and heart, and keep the line of communication open between us at all times. Help me to be patient, as you work out all things for my good.

Above all dear Lord, help me to let Your Love into my prayer life, so that I may grow in my relationship with you and be an example of Your Goodness to others. Amen.

Chapter 18

Forgiveness is giving up the hope that the past can be different.

~ Oprah Winfrey

What can you do to make the past change?

Nothing. You can't change the past. Yet we try by holding onto the events of our past in our mind, re-living painful situations and playing them over and over in our head. Thinking of the hurtful conversations again and again and continuing to dwell on them only gives the past more power over us. You cannot have that conversation again. But you can have a new one. A forgiving one.

I don't pretend that some of your situations aren't very serious or that your painful experiences weren't life changing. They were. But how has your life changed? Has refusing to forgive someone made your life better? I don't mean not having them in your life. I'm referring to the pain you carry around inside. Has it gone away because you've chosen not to forgive? These are questions only you can answer.

Healing has a timetable. But forgiveness doesn't. The time to forgive is now. This is easier said than done. Sometimes it feels like we shouldn't forgive because then we are condoning what they did to us, that it really wasn't so bad after all. No. It was bad. It was wrong. Forgiveness acknowledges this or there wouldn't be any need for it. By its very definition forgiveness says that something wrong was done ... but we can choose to let it go... completely.

Maybe we think that if we forgive someone we are letting them get away with something, so it's kind of like a crook we hold in the prison of our hearts so they can pay for their crime. The problem is we are the ones who get punished. It feels (and I stress *feels*) like they are suffering for what they did, when they're not. We are.

When we refuse to forgive - nothing happens to them. When we choose to forgive - nothing happens to them. It happens to us. So all things being equal, why not be free of it? You don't stop them from doing anything by staying angry. You stop yourself. Your thoughts do not control theirs. You can't "think them" into paying a price. They don't suffer because you do. They are free to, can, and will move on from this with or without you while you still try to ruin things for them in your mind. When you hang on to unforgiveness you are trying to make them feel bad and make yourself feel better, neither of which is happening.

It's time for us to accept reality. It's not working. We are controlling nothing. These thoughts of guilt we are trying to impose on them, are just our thoughts. When we persist in unforgiveness, we harm ourselves, and offend God.

There are many reasons to forgive others. For the Christian, the reason is pretty simple - Jesus told us to. He commanded us to. It's an order. That's a tough one to grasp. As Christians, we fail at forgiveness regularly. It's so hard. Much of what Jesus asks us to do is hard, which is why He offers us the grace to do it, making it easier. But too often we really don't want the grace, we want to stay mad. We hold on to it ... and it holds on to us.

As often as we fail, the important thing is to try. We need to pray and let God's grace in. We need to *want* to forgive, and then grace will come. On our own this is an incredible struggle, but with God *all things are possible.* The willingness to do it however, is up to us.

97

Even harder than forgiving others is probably forgiving yourself. Remember that you are loved and valued by God and He doesn't want you to punish yourself anymore either. Forgiving yourself sets you free and it sets the other person free too. In fact the process of coming to forgive yourself helps in learning to forgive others because you learn how faulted we *all* are.

Everyone makes mistakes. No one is perfect. Everyone says the wrong things. Everyone does thing they shouldn't do, and doesn't do things they should do. This is inevitable and we have done it too. We all have. Of course, some situations are easier to let go of than others. Hurt runs deep and everyone copes with hurt in different ways.

Some people are able to forgive more easily than others. Some people are sorry for their actions and some aren't. But the decision to forgive is an act of the will. We can choose what we do and say regardless of how we think or feel. Through prayer, what feels impossible can become a reality, and healing can occur - at least within ourselves.

Learning to forgive people who aren't sorry for their behavior is another big one, but the solution is the same, to forgive them regardless. While it would be ideal to talk things out and reconcile, it's not always possible. But we can still forgive them in our hearts, even without their apology. So don't wait for it. It may never come, and that's a lot of life to waste.

Above all, let's do what we expect others to. Let's be sure to seek forgiveness from others when we've hurt them as well. The work required of us on the inside will lend itself to forming a habit of forgiveness, where it will come a little more naturally to us as we learn to cooperate with God's grace.

"Therefore, as God's chosen people, holy and dearly loved, clothe yourselves with compassion, kindness, humility, gentleness and patience. Bear with each other and forgive one another if any of you has a grievance against someone. Forgive as the Lord forgave you." (Colossians 3:12-13)

We forgive, because Christ forgave us. He still forgives us, every day. He shed His Blood so that we can start over. We have received His Mercy, and now we are called to give it to others. With His help, we can let go of anger, be free of the past, and move forward in Love.

Reflection

Am I willing to talk with God about how deeply hurt I am?

What do I keep remembering about the person or situation?

Am I able to consider the other person's perspective?

Do I accept that they are also, like me, imperfect?

Am I angry or unforgiving toward myself?

Do I try to punish others by withholding forgiveness?

Do I believe in a God of Mercy?

Prayer

Dear Lord, only You know how hard it is for me to be the one to forgive here. This is what You want me to do, and my soul knows it, but please help me to do it. Nothing is beyond your power Lord and I need your power to do this. On my own I will stay angry forever but with You I can forgive everyone, including myself, and have a new life. I can be set free from this pain that controls me and this hurt that keeps me stuck in the past. Please help me to be willing to do what I have been so unwilling to do for so long.

Please help me to see this situation in a new light - Your light. Help me to be willing to see things differently, from an attitude of compassion and love, both for those who hurt me and for myself. Help me to love You enough, and myself enough, to let this go, not into thin air, but into your hands, your Heart. You will know how to bring Healing here.

Take the situation Lord. I give it to you now. Do whatever you want with it. It's not mine anymore. I let it go. I want something different. I want peace. I want healing. I want to be free.

Help me to always seek forgiveness from those that I hurt as well and above all, I thank You for forgiving me all of my sins and faults. Help me to not only ask You for Mercy but to also give Your Mercy to others, as I receive it for myself. Amen.

Chapter 19

"Even now," declares the Lord,

"Return to me with all your heart."

~ Joel 2:12

"Even now."

These are two of the greatest words in the whole Bible. *"Even now."* God is saying here, *"I don't care what you've done in the past, just come back to Me. Come back and be made well. Approach the throne of grace and receive Mercy from My hands"*. God can make right your wrongs. God can fix what you've broken. He can heal you and the people you've hurt. God can give you the grace to forgive yourself, no matter how horrible you may feel.

God just wants you back. This is His nature. It's just how He is - loving and forgiving. He doesn't want you to be stuck in the past. He wants you to be free. Free from shame, regret, remorse, and sin. We can't talk about becoming *"A New You"*, without talking about our need for God's Mercy in our own lives. It's what allows us to move forward towards the future in His grace.

When God says *"even now"*, He means it. These words sum up His incredible Mercy - it means "no matter what!" There is no scenario you can present to God that He wouldn't forgive. None! God loves you and will never reject you. Listen to that again. God loves you, and He will never reject you.

The problem we sometimes encounter with God's Mercy is that we don't deserve it. Well, let that be a problem no more - We don't! We don't deserve God's forgiveness. It's a free gift He's happy to give us. We can't earn it, and we can't pay it back. No amount of time or pain can make us worthy to receive grace. Accepting this, is the key to receiving it.

God is merciful to all and that means us. Yes, God will forgive us. Let's make a move - going to confession, seeking forgiveness from someone, praying more - let's take a step in the right direction, one that will restore us. With God's Mercy comes Healing. Confessing your sins to Jesus allows His Spirit to come to you in a New Way, and by His grace, fill you with a New Life, one where your past is no longer your present. A life where our sins are gone, washed away, and grace is poured out.

Christ's blood that was shed on the Cross for us is the only worthy and acceptable sacrifice, so let's stop trying to earn His forgiveness. It's already been won. But we must approach God, even now, and confess humbly our sorrow and sincere desire not to commit these sins again. Sin is real, and it's destructive, and God wants to help us avoid it. Will we fail? Yes, of course. But we will have a merciful God ready to greet us once again - and again, and He will never get tired of forgiving us.

God wants to be with you. God knows what your past has done to you and He knows what others have done to your past. He knows the longer you live in the past, the less time you spend with Him, because He's not there. God is in the present moment. God's mercy is available to us here, now. There is no need to wait another minute. We can even stop reading for a second, and talk to the Lord in this moment, telling Him what's on our hearts. He's listening and He knows what we need to hear.

Jesus came to give us a New Life! When we refuse God's Mercy we are pretty much telling Jesus that His sacrifice was a waste of time. That all of His suffering was for nothing. When we refuse forgiveness, we commit a sin of pride. If God is willing to forgive us, who are we to say no, that He is wrong to do so? We are all unworthy of His great Love and endless mercy, so let's stop trying to be worthy of it.

Let's accept the Love that is waiting for us. Let's ask Christ to come into our hearts and make them brand new. Let's be humble enough to admit we really do need His help in life and we need His forgiveness. God has already told us He wants to erase our past and start over. Let's say yes to God and finally let Him.

There is nothing God won't forgive. Our Loving Father knows our weaknesses and all of our sins, and He can't love us any more than He does right now. He is Love. And Love desires only to Love. We have a God inviting us to come close to Him, to come just as we are.

God also says to us here in this scripture to come "with *ALL* of your heart." Not some of your heart, or most of your heart - all of it. One hundred percent! Too often in prayer we bring to God our false self. We come to God as if He didn't create us and doesn't know what we're made of. We approach God with a ten foot pole - on the surface ready to "surrender" our lives to Him, but in reality not even willing to hand Him the pole. We come to God in prayer in a certain way, the way *we* want to. We present ourselves to God in a particular light, our own. Keeping this and that to the side, allowing Him only to touch the surface of our heart, while we do all the talking.

Hiding ourselves from God is not only counterproductive, it's also exhausting. The energy it takes to prevent God from finding out about us - that we have sinned, that we are filled with pride, that we are wounded, that we are angry, that we have a dream in our hearts, that we wished our lives were different, and the biggest secret of all - that we so desire to be loved and accepted! It takes a lot of emotional strain to try to disguise ourselves. It's tiresome. Come instead and let Jesus *"give you rest."*

Reflection

What area of my life am I trying to hide from God?

What is it that prevents me from giving God all of my heart?

Are there certain things I think are unforgiveable?

Do I think I have nothing to be sorry for?

Am I willing to confess my sins and seek forgiveness?

Prayer

Dear Lord, only you know the condition of my heart. You alone, know every tear, every sin, every desire. You know how much I long to be loved, unconditionally. You are my God. You created me and you know everything about me. I believe that you are Merciful and Good, yet I still avoid you for some reason.

I steer clear of talking to you about certain things. I know you will accept me just as I am and that I should approach you in prayer confident that you will Love me no matter what, but I find it difficult to be myself with you. Maybe I don't like myself too much, or maybe I'm afraid you will reject me. Please help me to understand that your Love is not like human love - it doesn't set conditions and it doesn't have any requirements that I have to meet first. I am free to come to you just as I am.

Lord I am truly sorry for my sins, for all the ways I have offended you and others. I pray for the grace to make a good confession and for Your help in becoming a better person. I ask you Father, in Jesus name, to set me free. I don't want to live in the dark anymore. I want the Light of Your Life in mine. You are The Way, The Truth, and The Life and I ask you to shine Your Light in my life and in my heart and help me to see more clearly, and believe more deeply, just how Merciful and Loving you really are. Amen.

Chapter 20

"Be who God meant you to be

and you will set the world on fire."

~ *St. Catherine of Siena*

Your real self. You know the one. The one we don't let others see because we're afraid of rejection. The one we keep to ourselves because we're sure we're going to fail. The one we try to hide from God because we think He will withdraw His Love from us, if He knew the real us.

Well God already knows the real us. He created us, and He created us *on purpose*! He has a plan for our lives and it doesn't include us trying to become someone else. God has an intention. By nature, He is creative and He has something in mind for us. Our job is to discover what that is, and lovingly enough, He allows this discovery to take place in relationship with Him. He wants us to know who we are, and we do this by getting to know Him.

We are made in the image and likeness of God. When we look at God we will see our own reflection. God is our Father, and as His children there will be a resemblance. But rather than looking closely at Him, we instead avoid Him. We have a sort of surface relationship with our Heavenly Father. Maybe even as faithful Christians we still see Jesus as the nice one and God the

Father as the "mean" one. This is false, and when our perception is off, everything we see will be cloudy.

Through prayer, we can come to know God as a Loving and protective Father, who never abandons His children. We will see His Love for us in the person of Jesus Christ, His Son. Jesus *is* The Father's Love. We will come to discover that God The Father is very much in all the details of our lives and wants so much for us to turn to Him for help and guidance throughout the day.

When we come to understand just how Good a Father He is and that He understands our weaknesses and Loves us anyway, we will begin to see our own reflection. That we too are lovable and good. That there is so much more to us than meets the eye.

Each of us are called to live out God's purpose for our lives, not someone else's. God has a plan for us to know Him better, but He also has a unique plan by which we can bring this knowledge to others. This is where we become, *"who God meant you to be"* as quoted above.

Through prayer and the study of scripture, we will learn what God is really like, and then He will want to use us to show others what He's like. This can take place in many ways, mainly by example. We are all called to bring His Healing Love into a broken world, but each will be called to do so in a unique way and with the unique people in our lives.

God knows best how to use us. We discover His Will through prayer. Not only vocal prayer, but silent prayer where we listen for His voice in our hearts. God can speak to us in many ways and point us in the right direction, but we need to be open to becoming the person *He* wants us to be, doing the things *He* wants us to do.

When we are really open to doing God's Will for *us*, and are less concerned about what He should be doing in others, change will occur. When we live out the life God wants us to live - we become New! When we allow God's grace to work in us, His grace will also flow through us to others. This is what it means to *"set the world on fire"* as quoted above. Not only will we be made new as we become the person God intends, but it will also create a spark in the people around us who experience God's Love *through* us. This spark will spread and continue to be passed along to others through them as well.

Bottom line, one person can change the world. And that one person is you!

Reflection

Do I believe God wants me to be Happy?

Am I willing to let go of my plans for God's plan for me?

Do I believe God made me for a reason?

Am I open to discovering what that reason is?

Do I believe God The Father, my Creator, Loves me?

Do I believe God has the power to make me New?

111

<u>Prayer</u>

Dear Heavenly Father, I thank you for revealing Your Love for me in the person of Your Son, Jesus Christ. I thank you for creating me, and I know that through Jesus I can have a brand new life and become a new creation! I want this new life. I know that only in You is my happiness to be found and I want to discover your plan for my life. Yet I am still so stuck on my own plans and can't seem to let go.

Please grant me the grace to surrender everything to you. Help me to be open to a New Way! Help me to Trust in Your Fatherly Goodness and Guidance. Help me to stay close to you in prayer as you reveal yourself to me more and more each day. Help me to become the person You want me to be. Help me to do the things you want me to do and say the things you want me to say. Help me to be less concerned with what others are doing and saying, and be more concerned that I don't miss any opportunities to bring Your Love to others. Amen.

A New You

Learning to let the past go into the arms of a loving God frees us to be ourselves - our real selves, where we are made new on the inside and are now able to reflect the image of Our Creator to the outside.

We have followed a pattern in this book, taking us through the process of becoming *A New You!* Beginning with God understanding and caring about our pain, followed by a new awakening of His great love for us. It is this Love that will transform us and make us new. This Love will allow us to trust Him and give Him our past, present and future. Next we focused on the fact that there is hope and that we can change. We can't change others but we can change ourselves. Living in the present moment opens wide the doors for this change. Finally we learn how to express this newness we've found by how we live our lives and treat others.

Becoming emotionally and spiritually healthy is worth the effort and prayer time we put into it. It also requires a holy self-love, self-acceptance, self-confidence, and self esteem. Accepting the *New You,* embracing the *New You*, and loving the *New You* is necessary to living the *New You.* Loving ourselves enough to let go and do the work of changing our behavior requires a rock solid foundation which can be found in God's Love for us. We will then be able to love ourselves, since we are made in His image and likeness. Healthy self-love stems from the humility of knowing who we are.

So who are you? You're a child of God. Why should you love yourself? Because you're a child of God. Why should others love you? Because you're a child of God. Why should you love others? Because you're a child of God. Why should you be happy? I will give you one guess.

Everything vital for healthy spirituality stems from who *God is*, not who we are. When we understand who He is and how much He loves us, we will, by default, understand our own worth and value as His children. We are irreplaceable.

The King of Glory Loves us. He lives within us, and He wants to be close with us. God Almighty has a very special place for us in His Heart, and He wants us to give Him a place in ours. The source of all things loves us. This is the heart of the matter.

God has a plan, and it's better than ours. His perspective is the right one. He has a much better view and He sees the whole picture. It's time to trust Him now. For those who once knew Him well, it's time to trust Him again.

Let's give God another opportunity to do wonderful things for us. Let's give Him a chance to put a new desire on our hearts. It's time to let go of what isn't going right. It's time to get to know Him better and ask Him for the grace to trust Him completely. It's time to be open to healing.

We have a God who can be known, who speaks to the center of our souls, the deepest areas of our hearts, a place where no one else can go. He's there. Right now.

God wants us to surrender our whole life to Him, a life He gave us. He wants us to have a fresh start with Him, a clean slate. He wants to free us from anxiety and fear, worry and depression, and all the things that keep us from living our life fully. He wants to free us from the past and give us hope. It's never too late to begin again.

It's your spiritual journey. No one can take it from you and no one can take it for you. But I hope this book encourages you to take it and to start from the top, not from a place of self, but from a place of Love. We can continue this path we're on by utilizing New Way Today's *"My New Way Journal"* and documenting our journey on a daily basis throughout the year. We can develop a plan, and take the steps we need to, one day at a time.

So finally, let's be open to our God of Love and Mercy, who desires to forgive us, heal us, and make us whole. A God who desires to refresh us and help us to change. We can have a new beginning and a new life. We don't have to live in the past anymore. We don't have to be the way we've always been. We can allow something new to come into our lives.

In a New Way let's open our heart Today and give God permission to kick start our life right now, even in this very moment. Let the *NEW YOU* begin.

115

<u>Prayer</u>

Dear Lord, I have come to the beginning of my journey. I thank you for being with me always. Thank you for guiding me through life and being a friend to me. Thank you for being so patient with me. Thank you that I can start over again and again at any minute, and you will never get tired of giving me chance after chance. Thank you that Your Love and Mercy are beyond my imagination.

Please give me Your Way of Living from now on. Please heal me and set me free from my broken past. Help me to let go and surrender and become the person You created me to be. I ask for a complete transformation of my heart and mind to You and Your plan for my life.

Every day is a new beginning. It doesn't matter to You what mistakes I made yesterday. What matters is that I keep trying and I continue to live in Your Presence. Please help me to start living my life in New Way, Today.

New Way Today

Visit www.newwaytoday.net for updated information, articles and inspirational prayers.

Also check out New Way Today's Page on Amazon.com

Please join us at facebook.com/NewWayToday for daily inspirational posts.

Just click "Like" and be a part of this page encouraging one another to live life in a New Way - Every Day!

May God Bless you and everyone near and dear to you.

Made in the USA
Lexington, KY
23 July 2014